My Muslim Friends
Have Been Lied To

But They Don't Know It

By

Gil VanOrder, Jr.

COPYRIGHT

MY MUSLIM FRIENDS HAVE
BEEN LIED TO

But They Don't Know It

By Gil VanOrder, Jr.

ISBN: 9798737011154

CONTENTS

PREFACE

I love all my Muslim friends. I try to communicate that in every way I can whenever I am with them. At the same time, I hurt for them and for every follower of Islam. Why? Because when I talk with them, I realize they have been lied to. Furthermore, they don't realize it. They have accepted a religious belief based on what they have been taught without knowing all the facts. My heart's desire in writing this book is to present to my Muslim friends enough new information to cause them to want to know more. I wish for them to have a better and more accurate understanding of both Islam and Christianity, so they can make an informed decision as to whom they should follow – Mohammed or Jesus – and why. If just one of my Muslim friends reads and is enlightened by this book, I will rejoice that I have written it.

CHAPTER 1: WHY AND HOW I CAME TO CARE

Let me begin this book by sharing why I became interested in those who believe in Islam. It all started when I was a young and naive youth worker back in 1980. I was raised in rural farm country. The number of students of color in my high school as well as the college I attended could be counted on one hand. As a result, I had zero experience working with minorities. In His infinite wisdom (and maybe sense of humor), God called me to work with black teenagers in a disadvantaged urban community in upstate New York. It was the kind of neighborhood where you could meet a teen one day and discover he was dead or in jail the next. To my surprise, I found many of the African American teens were members of a Muslim group called "The Five Percenters." The male adherents changed their "Christian slave names" to ones such as Tislam, Basheem, Rasheem, and Mohammed. They studied Islamic writings, including the Koran, hoping to attain a certain level of knowledge known as "120 degrees."

When a devotee reached this stage, he was then called "Allah." For urban youth with poor self-esteem, this was extremely attractive. They could become gods. As a result, it held a very strong grip in the community, especially among the teenagers.

In addition, I discovered that The Five Percenters were taught that they were the original race. Because black is the dominant gene and white the recessive gene, the first humans had to be black. Genetically, two recessive genes (white) could never produce a dominant gene (black). Two dominants, however, can produce a recessive if the parent dominants have the recessive genes as well. When a teen would ask me how I, as a white man, felt about coming from black ancestors, I responded that God created Adam from the dirt of the ground and not from a white sandy beach. Thus, I had no problem believing Adam and Eve may have been dark skinned. It made no difference to me. This wasn't the response they expected.

Furthermore, according to their teaching, white people came from black people as a result of an evil scientist named Yacub. When Yacub created white people about 6,000 years ago, it was actually the devil coming out of god. Thus, in their view, white people were devils to be killed. To make matters worse, followers were taught that it was not only okay to kill white people, but it was their sacred duty as members of The Five Percenters.

Unaware of this, at the time, I offered the teens a free week of camp if they would be willing to listen to my presentations of the Christian faith. They were interested in the fun of a camp experience, but not the "religious stuff." Nevertheless, a few boys agreed to attend. Most of their moms were glad to sign the consent forms, thankful for the week of respite.

By the end of that first week of camp I had learned a great deal about the boys and their faith, including the fact paradise for Muslim men would be one continuous sex orgy. When I asked the boys who the virgins were who would service them (e.g., their sisters, friends, daughters), they didn't know. Then I asked them if they thought this would be paradise for the female virgins. Apparently, they hadn't considered what women, including their moms, would do in heaven. It seemed they were only interested in the idea of satisfying their sexual appetites for all eternity. It was obvious to me their theology was not well thought out.

While playing softball on the last day of camp, one of the older boys calling himself Allah pushed one of the younger boys to the ground. Allah was upset with the twelve-year old for striking out at bat. When I told the sixteen-year-old we didn't behave that way at camp, he immediately punched me in the face, sending me reeling. I was stunned. This wasn't exactly what I had in mind when I went into youth work! When I collected myself, I realized he was coming at me with fists raised. As he swung at me again, I dove into his legs knocking him to the ground. My high school wrestling experience enabled me to get him into a position where he could no longer bite me. Now he could only spit in my face. He kept yelling, "Get this white boy off me." Fortunately, none of the other boys jumped in or we would have had a riot on our hands.

I told him if he settled down, I would let him up, but he had to "chill out." He finally agreed. I let him up and he ran into the woods only to return with a huge stick (more like a long log). He swung it at me and I ducked, just in time to avoid a clubbing to the left side of my head. I could hear the swish as the branch whizzed over me. I dove into the boy's legs for the second time and tackled him to the ground. One of the other counselors took the stick away while I pinned him down again.

Amazingly, during the entire episode, I remained extraordinarily calm. Normally in a situation like this, the adrenaline would be pumping and one would become extremely excited, thus I knew my peace was the presence of God the Holy Spirit. I remember asking God over and over throughout this ordeal, "God, why are You allowing this to happen? How can You be glorified in this?" I couldn't see then what purpose all this violence could serve.

Knowing I couldn't hold this boy down forever, I looked for an excuse to let him up. At this point, he yelled, "When we get back to Albany, man, I'm going to kill you." I quickly responded, "I tell you what—if you agree to wait until we get back to Albany to kill me, I'll let you up. But you've got to agree that this is it for here." He said he agreed.

Actually, he said, *word,* which is supposed to signify they're telling the absolute truth. *Word* is short for *word bond.*

So, I let him up. Dumb! As soon as he got to his feet, he took off his belt and started whacking me with the buckle. He tore my shirt and ripped open a gash on the side of my neck. Without hesitation, I pulled off my own belt and held it buckle end down. Realizing the odds were now even, he backed off. I was grateful because I certainly didn't want to have to strike him.

He walked off to another part of the camp. One of the other counselors agreed to follow him. I asked the counselor to let him "chill out" for a while before talking to him. I was hoping we would be able to shake hands in peace before we left the camp. The counselor later told me it was not going to happen. The teen was intent on killing me once we returned to Albany.

Camp ended without further incident and we took the boys home. Before dropping them off, we told them we were starting a weekly club program at the local community center if they wanted to attend.

Before the evening of our first club meeting, I had called every prayer warrior I knew. I had two concerns in going back to the Arbor Hill section of Albany. One was obviously that this boy would be waiting for me with a knife or a gun. The second was that the staff at the community center would not permit us to use their facilities, as previously arranged, when they heard about what happened at camp. After all, what kind of youth workers physically fight with kids.

Upon arriving at the center, several staff members approached me and said they had heard about my fight with Allah. The other boys told them that I had Allah on the ground and could have punched his lights out, but didn't. "Instead, Gil just held him there even though Allah punched, bit, kicked, and spit on Gil," they related in apparent astonishment.

I was prepared for bad news, but instead every staff person said basically the same thing: "We understand you believe in that 'turn-the-other-cheek' idea, but you really should have beaten some sense into that kid." While I did not agree with their philosophy, I was grateful to know the incident had not affected our arrangement for a meeting place, and thankful to have been able to restrain Allah without having to return his blows.

My second concern was addressed when Allah walked into that first meeting with a two-liter bottle of Mountain Dew in his hands. At first, I thought he was planning to use it as a weapon. To my surprise, he offered the bottle to me. A number of questions went through my mind at that moment. The one thing I was sure of, however, was that this was a peace offering. I accepted his offer and took a big swallow, saying a quick prayer against any potential health hazards. Allah and I were on friendly terms from that time on.

Allah's attitude was not the only thing that changed. As a direct result of the camp experience, there was a change in all the boys' attitudes. They began to actually listen to what I was saying. It was almost as if they felt, "If Gil is willing to go through all he did, he must have something pretty important to say." I now knew why God allowed the camp episode to happen. I had earned the right to be heard. I would not want to have to go through it ever again (and I never did in all the subsequent years I worked there), but it was necessary to gain the guys' respect. It was clear from then on, that the adults were in charge and not the teens. Thank God, we were never again challenged in that way. As a result of starting this ministry, we ended up establishing three girls' clubs and three guys' clubs, and God used it to change the lives of many inner-city young people. God took evil and turned it to good.

The Five Percenters have since changed their name to "The Nation of Gods and Earth." Prior to that it had become a major element in the lyrics of rap music. L.L. Cool J's Five Percent name was Lord Supreme Shalik. In his book, *I Make My Own Rules*, he says being a Five Percenter was "nothing more than a license to be brutal." Tupac Shakur, Queen Latifah, Rakim, Brand Nubian and other gangsta rappers were all involved with The Five Percenters, and their music reflected those beliefs. While The Nation of Gods and Earth's theology contains a great deal of Muslim influence and requires the reading of the Koran, it is obviously not the same as the major religion of Islam as it is practiced worldwide today.

The reason I tell this story is because it was this experience that caused me to wonder if the followers of Islam had any of the same flaws in what they believed as did The Five Percenters. If they did, then I knew, if I cared at all about others, that I was obligated to help them see where these flaws existed. So, I first set out to learn as much as I could about this particular religion. I had taken courses in college on world religions, but now I read the Koran and studied books that dealt with Islam. Most importantly, I began to listen to what my Muslim friends would say they believed. The more I learned, the sadder I became as I realized how little understanding these devoted followers had about history and other religions. Most were capable of explaining what they had been taught was true, but all recited far more misinformation than actual facts.

The first clue I had that there were false teachings being circulated was when I heard a very loud Muslim scream, "The Bible copied the writings of the Koran!" But that is easily proven to be wrong. Every credible historian knows the Bible was written well before the Koran. The Koran was not written until after 600 A.D. Manuscripts of the Gospels – to say nothing of the Old Testament – have been discovered that pre-date by hundreds of years even the earliest manuscripts of the Koran. One papyrus fragment from the book of Mark is called the "John Rylands Manuscript," also known as "P52," and dates back to 130AD. Clearly, the writers of the Bible could not have copied from the Koran. Just the opposite is possible, however, due to the Koran's much later date and the fact Mohammad had access to the New Testament Scriptures.

Despite the abundance of evidence to the contrary, many Muslims hold to the belief that the Bible was written after the Koran. This is not the only falsehood they refuse to reject as I will share later. For now, I must regrettably tell readers there are two kinds of doubts (honest and dishonest). An honest doubter says, "Show me the evidence and I will believe." Unfortunately, most Muslims are dishonest doubters who say, "I won't believe regardless of the evidence." Thus, it becomes extremely difficult to convince them of the truth.

CHAPTER 2: THE KORAN AND THE BIBLE

I approach a discussion of the two holy books, the Koran and the Bible, with a great deal of caution. I realize that followers of Islam take offense at anyone who would question the Koran. I have no interest in offending anyone, but I think it only fair to consider both the Bible and the Koran in terms of their claims. Muslims, of course, believe the Koran is more reliable and factual than the Bible. So, I will begin with some information regarding the Bible and explain the ways it differs from the Koran.

Before I do that, I want to point out that Muslims are far more diligent in their study of and knowledge of what their religious book teaches. Sadly, many people who would call themselves Christians have very little knowledge of the Bible. Unlike my Muslim friends, these so called "Christians" do not take their holy book seriously enough to read it on a regular basis or, more importantly, learn from what they read. Such shallow believers may even argue that the Bible is true without having actually read it.

Additionally, our once Christian nation no longer teaches the Bible in its public schools as it once did. This is not true for the education of Muslims. They are taught the Koran from a very early age and continue to be taught throughout their lives. They are to be admired for their faithful devotion to religious instruction.

At one time our nation taught Christian beliefs to every child in America. English was taught in grade school by using such Christian textbooks as *The McGuffey Reader*. Daily Bible reading and prayer was the normal practice by teachers throughout the country's schools. Today, the Bible isn't even allowed to be read in our county's public schools. Far worse, is the attempt by many educators to actually denounce the Bible claiming it to be a bunch of myths, folklore, and contradictions. Rather than encouraging students to read the Bible, college professors want their pupils to view the Bible as unfit for consumption by an intelligent mind. This has resulted in a generation of students ignorant of a book that is annually purchased by more people than any other book ever written in all the world.

This ignorance by current students was perfectly illustrated on April 4, 2020, on an episode of Jeopardy's College Championship. Only the brightest of students are picked to participate in this quiz show. One young man from Northwestern University made it all the way to the semi-finals. He demonstrated a great deal of knowledge on just about every subject presented except one – the Bible. One of the answers he was asked to respond to was "After he returns, in Luke 15, his Dad says, 'Bring hither the fatted calf, and kill it, and let us be merry.'" The student responded by saying, "Who is Cain?" Not only did he not know the story of the Prodigal Son, but it appears he thought the New Testament book of Luke is where the story of Cain and Able is found.

This college student is not unique in his ignorance of the Bible. Ask almost any college student today a question such as, "Who wrote the Gospels?" and you will receive a blank stare. They will be clueless. They may not even know how many Gospels there are to say nothing of having read one. That is because they have been duped into believing the Bible is not credible. It would be unfair, however, to assume these students are committed Christians even if they might identify themselves as such. But it is fair for Muslim to view such "Christians" as shallow and ignorant of their own faith, because they are. Nevertheless, one should not judge the credibility of a particular faith based on the ignorance of some who claim to follow it.

One should judge a faith on the basis of its origin, its teachings, and how sound it is. The origin of Christianity, of course, is traced back to Christ. The teachings are recorded in the Bible. So, it is imperative that we examine what the Bible records and investigate those records, as best we can, to determine if they are reliable. It is interesting to note that many (including atheistic lawyers) have attempted to study the Bible with the intent of disproving the Bible but have, after close examination, become believers instead. On what basis have these former sceptics been convinced the Bible is accurate? Consider the following evidences:

The Bible is historically accurate.

One of the ways scholars determine the accuracy of an historical account is by comparing it with other accepted historical writings from the same time period. Based on all the other information we have from the various time periods described in the Bible, it is not hyperbole to say the Bible is completely trustworthy in its recording of history. It can be relied upon to give very detailed accounts of what took place at the times being described, including what countries existed, who was king or ruler over them, what customs people practiced, and any number of other historical facts. Nothing has been found showing the Bible recorded something that contradicts known facts of history.

Extensive examination has discovered only a small number of potential discrepancies in the Bible, but they are minor ones probably due to human transcription errors. Despite the early transcribers meticulous efforts to duplicate every word and punctuation mark exactly, there are a few possible small mistakes. For example, I Kings 4:26 says Solomon had 40,000 horses while II Chronicles 9:25 says he only had 4,000. There are many explanations offered for these kinds of differences but the most logical is that a zero was left out in copying the number. Perhaps, due to excessive wear a zero was worn off from the original text. Whatever the situation, there was no doctrine violated or lost in the translation. It may even be that the count was taken at two different times during Solomon's lifetime. Maybe one was taken early in his reign as king and the other toward the end of his reign. But the most likely explanation appears to be that it was an error made by someone in translating the original text.

These small errors in copying represent mistakes made by humans despite their best efforts. While the original writings were perfect in every way because they came from God, when man got involved in writing the originals over, they made a few minor mistakes. Not a single one of these transcription errors, however, affects any of the truth taught. In other words, there are no theological contradictions. Everything the Bible teaches is consistent and without mistakes.

One might ask why God would allow man to make any mistakes in translating the Bible. The answer may well be because He knew if the Bible were totally perfect in every way, some would worship the book rather than Him or, at least, along with Him. Men have a tendency to want to worship things they can see rather than God whom they cannot see. That's why the Bible warns against worshiping idols. If idols made by human hands are worshipped, imagine how much more attractive a perfect book from God would be worshipped. Regardless of the reason, we know we can trust all the Bible's teachings. The discovery of writings such as the Dead Sea Scrolls have shown just how accurate our current Bible is to all the very earliest copies and manuscripts. No truth has been altered so there are no theological contradictions. Overall, even the transcriptions are close to perfect.

It is for this reason Christians do not fear critical examination of their Holy Book. Unlike Muslims, who have killed those who have questioned the Koran, Christians eagerly encourage skeptics to read the Bible with a critical eye – the closer the scrutiny the better. Truth has no reason to fear tough examination. Christians know that honest inquiry can lead to faith. Many former atheists and agnostics have become Christians as a result of studying the evidence. Some initially began their investigation in an attempt to disprove the Bible but discovered the truth to be undeniable. A few notable individuals who have turned from atheism to belief include:

Kirk Cameron - Actor, star of *Growing Pains*
Whittaker Chambers - Former Communist
Francis Collins - physician-geneticist and the director of the National Human Genome Research Institute
Larry Darby - Former Holocaust denier

and member of the American Atheists
Peter Hitchens - Brother of late
outspoken atheist Christopher
Hitchens Khang Khek Leu (also known
as Comrade Duch) – Cambodian
director of Phnom Penh's infamous
Tuol Sleng detention center
C.S. Lewis - Oxford professor and
writer
Alister McGrath - Biochemist and
Christian theologian. Founder of
'Scientific Theology' and critic of
atheist Richard Dawkins
William J. Murray - author and son of
atheist activist Madalyn Murray
O'Hair
Bernard Nathanson Medical doctor who
performed thousands of abortions
and was a founding member of
NARAL, later becoming a Pro-Life
proponent
Marvin Olasky - Former Marxist turned
Christian conservative, he edits the
Christian World Magazine
Rosalind Picard - Director of the
Affective Computing Research Group
at the MIT Media Lab
George R. Price - Geneticist
Aleksandr Solzhenitsyn - Nobel Prize

winning author

Lee Strobel - Author of *The Case For Christ*

The writers were honest.

Another way that scholars determine the accuracy of an historical account is by examining the trustworthiness of the authors. Whether the historians are writing about what happened to George Washington, Napoleon, or Ayatollah Khomeini, they must be considered honest reporters before any confidence is placed in the truth of what they have written. Therefore, it is imperative that one scrutinize the writers of the Bible. But before we examine the honesty of the biblical writers, it is worth noting how many writers there were. Unlike the Koran, where we are asked to trust the writings of just on individual, the Bible was written by forty different authors from many different backgrounds, many different cultures, and over many different time periods separated by thousands of years. Yet, despite this extreme diversity, the Bible is a congruent story of how God has chosen to act in history and how he has revealed himself to humankind. There are no contradictions between what one author states and what any of the other authors state. This in itself is amazing, if not miraculous, and gives evidence of the trustworthiness of the writers of both the Old and New Testaments.

But how can we be sure we can trust the writers, especially those of the New Testament? One reason is because they were eyewitnesses to the occurrences. The author of the book of Acts, for example, claimed he was there at the time of Christ and saw what happened. He wrote, "God has raised this Jesus to life, and we are all witnesses of it" (Acts 2:32). He also wrote, "We are witnesses of everything he did in the country of the Jews and in Jerusalem. They killed him by hanging him on a cross, but God raised him from the dead on the third day and caused him to be seen. He was not seen by all the people, but by witnesses whom God had already chosen—by us who ate and drank with him after he rose from the dead" (Acts 10:39-41).

John, the Apostle, also tells us he was a witness to Jesus along with many others. John wrote, "We proclaim to you what we have seen and heard" (I John 1:3). What happened was recorded by those who were there at the time including fishermen like John, a doctor named Luke, and Paul, a one-time hater of Christians. There were also other historians, whose words are not found in the Bible, who recorded some of the acts of Jesus.

Doubters have suggested the writers were either delusional or just plain dishonest. If they were delusional there are several questions that have to be asked. How is it possible so many people hallucinated the same thing at different times? Why didn't a single contemporary ever make such a claim about these witnesses? How is it possible none of the writers showed any signs normally associated with individuals not dealing in reality? All the writers were lucid and clear in their writings. Where is there found any evidence to suggest they were delusional?

If the writers were sane but dishonest in their reporting, what was their motive? It certainly wasn't for personal glory. They portrayed themselves as ignorant, lacking in faith, sinful, and often inept. If they were lying about the events that took place, it seems likely they would also lie about themselves and record how good they were as disciples. The fact they didn't gives indication they were being honest in what they wrote.

The ultimate test of their reliability is found in their willingness to die for the risen Lord they wrote about. If the whole story were just a fictitious tale, why would they be willing to be tortured for it? They must have believed it was true. Otherwise, at least one of them would have "spilled the beans" especially just before he was to be beheaded. What's the point of being a martyr for what you know is a hoax?

Furthermore, there were other historical writers of the time who were not followers of either the Jewish religion or of Christianity who recorded the existence of Jesus. There are more than 6,000 manuscripts (including secular ones) that record the existence of a person named Jesus. In fact, there is more evidence for the existence of Jesus than there is for any other individual in all of antiquity. There are very few manuscripts, for example, that indicate there once was a man named Plato, yet we have no trouble believing he existed. Why then (with the superior evidence available for Christ's existence) do people claim Jesus was a myth or a fable? The problem of acceptance isn't found in any inaccuracies of the historical records. The inability of people to trust the records is primarily due to their unwillingness. People do not want to believe the Biblical record despite the abundance of evidence. Their doubts are dishonest doubts.

The Bible is prophetically accurate.

In addition to its historical accuracy, the Bible is also true prophetically. No prophecy given in the Bible has ever turned out to be wrong. This alone should make a believer out of the most adamant skeptic. Even though there is no doubt all the Old Testament prophecies were written hundreds of years before the New Testament fulfillment of them, every one of them turned out to be correct. To be 100 percent accurate in predicting future events is more than just improbable, it is impossible apart from an omniscient God. Compare 100% to the success rate of secular predictions.

A study of psychics in 1975 and observed until 1981 showed that of the seventy-two predictions, only six were fulfilled in any way. Two of these were vague and two others were hardly surprising – the U.S. and Russia would remain leading powers and there would be no world wars. The People's Almanac (1976) did a study of predictions of twenty-five top psychics. The results: Of the total seventy-two predictions, sixty-six (92%) were totally wrong. An accuracy rate around 8 percent could easily be explained by chance and general knowledge of circumstances. In 1993 the psychics missed every major unexpected news story, including Michael Jordan's retirement, the Midwest floods, and the

Israel-PLO peace treaty. Among the false prophecies were that the Queen of England would become a nun and Kathie Lee Gifford would replace Jay Leno as host of "The Tonight Show" (*Charlotte Observer*, 12/30/93).

Old Testament prophets, on the other hand, had to be 100% accurate because they were stoned if any of their prophecies failed (Deuteronomy 18:20). Of the hundreds of Old Testament prophecies, not a single error has been found. The odds of even a half dozen predictions happening exactly as foretold is beyond comprehension. Neither the ability of man nor simple chance can account for such perfection in knowing the future. Note, for example, the dates of the following prophecies concerning Jesus and then the dates of their New Testament fulfillments.

PROPHECY	B.C. DATE/ WRITTEN BY	A.D. DATE/ RECORDED BY
Be born in Bethlehem	700B.C./ Micah 5:2	60-65A.D./ Matthew 2:1-6 circa 60/ Luke 2:1-20

Be born of a virgin	740-680/ Isaiah 7:14	60-65/ Matthew 1:18-25 circa 60/ Luke 1:26-38
Enter Jerusalem in triumph	520-518/ Zechariah 9:9	60-65/ Matthew 21:1-9 85-90/ John12:12-16
Be rejected by his own people	740-680/ Isaiah 53:1,3 circa 1000/ Psalm 118:22	60-65/ Matthew 26:3, 4 85-90/ John 12:37-43 61-70/(Luke) Acts 4:1-12
Be betrayed by one of His followers	circa 1000/ Psalm 41:9	60-65/ Matt. 26:14-16; 26: 47-50 circa 60/ Luke 22:19-23
Be tried and condemned	740-680/ Isaiah 53:8	60-65/ Matthew 27:1, 2 circa 60/ Luke 23:1-25
Be silent before His accusers	740-680/ Isaiah 53:7	60-65/ Matt. 27:12-14 55-65/ Mark15:3-4 circa 60/ Luke 23:8-10
Be struck and spat upon by his enemies	740-680/ Isaiah 50:6	60-65/ Matt. 6:67; 27:30 55-65/ Mark 14:65

Be mocked and taunted	circa 1000/ Psalm 22:7, 8	60-65/ Matt. 27:39-44 circa 60/ Luke 23:11, 35
Die by crucifixion	circa 1000/ Psalm 22:14, 16, 17	60-65/ Matt. 27:31 55-65/ Mark 15:20, 25
Suffer with criminals and pray for his enemies	740-680/ Isaiah 53:12	60-65/ Matt. 27:38 55-65/ Mark 15:27, 28
Be given vinegar and gall	circa 1000/ Psalm 69:21	60-65/ Matt. 27:34 85-90/ John 19:28-30
Lots cast for his garments	circa 1000/ Psalm 22:18	60-65/ Matt. 27:35 85-90/ John 19:23, 24
No bones ever broken	1445-1405/ Exodus 12:46	85-90/ John 19:31-36
A sacrifice for sin	740-680/ Isaiah 53:5 6, 8, 10-12	85-90/ John 1:29; 11:49-52
Rise from the dead	circa 1000/ Psalm 16:10	60-65/ Matt. 28:1-10 61-70/(Luke) Acts 2:22-32

Skeptics, of course, try to argue that the New Testament writers simply wrote the history of Jesus in a way that would fulfill the earlier prophecies. But such a suggestion fails on a number of counts. First, there was no reason for the writers to do that. If anything, the incentive was not to do so. The religious leaders not only rejected the idea that Jesus was the predicted Messiah, but they ridiculed, imprisoned, and even tortured those who thought He was. Even the disciples were unsure as to whether or not Jesus was who He said He was. They would not have tried to convince themselves of His authenticity by falsifying the facts. Just the opposite occurred. The facts were what convinced them He was, indeed, the Messiah.

Additionally, if they had created false narratives about Jesus, no one living at the time would have believed them. They would have been easily exposed and laughed at. Yet, thousands of people became followers of Christ based on what the disciples said about Him.

Furthermore, there is no record of anyone producing evidence that disproves what Jesus did or that the disciples made up stories about Christ to fit every single prophecy given about the Messiah. There were even non-believers who recorded that Jesus did what the disciples claimed He did.

Finally, there are too many other prophecies in the Bible that cannot be explained away by suggesting later writers corrupted their recorded history in order to make the prophecies come true. For example, the Jews were told they would be disbursed from their homeland into all the other countries of the world (Ezekiel 22:15). According to the experts, Ezekiel was written between 593-560 B.C. It wasn't until 70 A.D. (hundreds of years after the prediction was made) this prophecy came true. Historians of all stripes recorded this to be true. The Bible also predicted the Jews would ultimately return to their homeland. This prophecy was made by several Old Testament writers including Amos (Amos 9:14-15) written in 755 B.C. Prior to 1948 A.D. no one even imagined the Jews would come together from the far corners of the globe and form the new country of Israel. Yet, that is exactly what happened over 2,000 years after it was predicted in the Bible. There are people still living today who can verify that is what occurred.

Only one book from all antiquity – the Bible – has ever made hundreds of prophecies that were 100% accurate. How is this possible if it is simply the writings of mere mortals? Only God knows the future with absolute certainty. Only He could be flawless in making so many predictions.

Allow me to make one other observation regarding Biblical prophecies. There are many prophecies in the Bible that have not yet been fulfilled. These deal primarily with what will happen during the end times. What is fascinating about them is that some of them are already starting to come to pass. For example, the Bible tells us that in the end times everyone will be required to have an ID put either on their forehead or hand. Without such a mark, a person will not be able to buy or sell (see Revelation 13:16-17). This prophecy was made thousands of years before anyone could have even imagined such a thing as a microchip.

Currently, with the coronavirus pandemic, there is a great deal of discussion regarding the need for such a global form of ID. Scientists want to be able to determine who you are, where you are, and with whom you have had personal contact in order to control the spread of the virus.

When such a form of universal identification takes place, few will recognize that it was all prophesied centuries before it actually was undertaken.

The Bible also tells us that eventually everyone will unite as one under a world government. Already, there are globalists attempting to bring such a world government into being. Because of the many wars, famines, and global pandemics (also prophesied) such a concept will become attractive worldwide. Again, all these things were foretold long before anyone could even conceive of them happening. There are numerous prophecies that a biblically literate person will understand whereas a biblically illiterate person will not.

The Bible is archeologically accurate.

A third way the Bible is accurate is archeologically. As in the two previous areas, the Bible has been found to be 100% reliable here as well. There has never been an archeological discovery that showed the Bible to be wrong. World-class archaeologists from around the world, including Millar Burrows of Yale, William F. Albright, and Sir William Ramsey have all studied the biblical records and concluded the same thing. Professor F. F. Bruce noted that "archaeology has confirmed the New Testament record."[1] Archaeologist Nelson Glueck has boldly asserted: "It may be stated categorically that no archaeological discovery has ever controverted a biblical reference. Scores of archaeological findings have been made which confirm in clear outline or exact detail historical statements in the Bible."[2] Dr. Joseph P. Free stated: "Archaeology has confirmed countless passages which have been rejected by critics as unhistorical or contradictory to known facts. Yet, archaeological discoveries have shown that these critical charges are wrong and that the Bible is trustworthy in the very statements which have been set aside as untrustworthy. We do not know of any cases where the Bible has been proved wrong."[3] To this day, archeologists continue to discover findings that validate the Biblical record.

The Bible is experientially accurate.

For centuries, men and women have discovered experientially that the Bible is trustworthy. In it they have found the truth that has led them to the hope, love, and guidance they had previously been unable to find anywhere else. Many were living lives in futility and despair until they began believing in and following the Bible. Afterwards, they report finding satisfaction never before realized. They testify to discovering a life more abundant than they could have ever imagined. Are these millions of people all delusional? If so, I am one of them. Like so many others, I have not only found the Scriptures to be true, but God to be faithful in answering my prayers. He has even performed miracles in order to meet my needs. One of the most amazing miracles He performed took place during my college years.

In the summer of 1970, after the spring planting season was over, I was laid off at the local Agway store where I had been working while attending college. There simply wasn't enough work to justify keeping me on, despite the fact my wife and I had a newborn baby and no other source of income. To make matters worse, the rent was due and we didn't have any money to pay it. While our small apartment wasn't much, it was all we had. But the $70 monthly charge in 1970 might as well have been $10 million as far as our ability to pay was concerned. We had a mountain of financial troubles at that time.

The rent was due Monday, and it was now Sunday evening. We had no known source of relief available to us except one. We decided to pray together for a miracle from God. We had nowhere else to turn. So together we knelt down beside the living room couch and prayed for $70. It was a very emotional time for us, and we both found ourselves crying as we got up from our knees. As we sat back down on the couch, still wiping the tears from our eyes, there was a knock on the door. It was late and so we looked at each other wondering who would be visiting us at such an hour.

The visitor introduced himself as Tom Thompson. He asked me if my name was Gil, and if I remembered meeting Tom at a Bible study weeks earlier. I said I was indeed Gil, but I was sorry to say I couldn't remember meeting Tom. Tom said that was okay. The important thing was that Tom had remembered me. Tom explained how he was a donor to a number of national and international Christian organizations, including Billy Graham, World Vision, and others. But lately he sensed God was telling him he needed to give more locally. So, while continuing to give to these other organizations, he was praying about where he should give more money right here in his own home town of Wellsville, New York. He went on to explain that every time he prayed about where he should give and to whom, my name came up. He said, "I pray and I think of you." I expressed surprise, especially because I didn't even remember meeting Tom.

Again, Tom said that didn't matter because God was more concerned that Tom remembered me. He said, "I have no idea what your financial situation is right now, Gil, but I feel God wants me to give you this tonight" and he handed me a check for $70. It was *exactly* what we had prayed for; *exactly* what we needed to pay our rent the next day. Needless to say, this started my wife and me crying again. As we explained our story to Tom, tears welled up in his eyes. He knew then he had indeed heard God correctly and had obediently responded to His leading.

Throughout our life together, my wife and I have experienced God's miraculous provision on numerous occasions. Multitudes of others say the same thing. We certainly are not unique in knowing the Lord is a miracle worker and wonderful provider. The Bible is true when it says that "God shall supply all your need according to his riches." (Philippians 4:19)

Skeptics may contend that Tom's arrival was simply coincidence. I find that harder to believe than to believe in God. To suggest it was simply luck that Tom arrived exactly when he did (right after we had prayed and just before the rent was due), chose me out of all the people in town he could have given money to (a population of thousands), gave me exactly the amount I was praying for ($70), and remembered my name after meeting me only once (and without even knowing I had a financial need) stretches the laws of probability beyond any honest measure.

When I told this story to a friend of mine, he suggested I write up the story and submit it to *Guidepost Magazine* for publication. I did and received a letter from the magazine's editor stating they receive so many of these types of letters they could not use any more including mine. What he was saying to me was my extraordinary experience was common place. So many have had similar stories to tell that he had an overabundance of them. I now tell people who suggest such miraculous happenings are merely coincidental they may be right, but I find the more I pray, the more these coincidences happen.

The Bible is scientifically accurate.

This will no doubt surprise some, but the Bible has also been found to be 100% accurate scientifically on everything it has to say about scientific matters. Granted, when it tells of God's intervention into the laws of nature (i.e., He performs miracles such as walking on water) He often defies the normal laws found in creation. That is not the same, however, as making statements about the laws of nature themselves. It is understandable that God can change the laws of nature given the fact He is the one who created them in the first place. He certainly has the right and the power to change them if He should choose to do so. If He could not, He would not be the sovereign God. The point is, apart from these special interventions of God, nothing stated in the Bible about nature has been proven to be contrary to the known laws of science.

One might argue that there are some contradictions between what the Bible says and some of the "theories" of science (theories which cannot be proven). The most obvious one being the theory of macroevolution. But more recent scientific research has found evidence to dispute many of these theories, especially the theory of macroevolution. It is not the intention of this book to go into all of the significant findings, but there are numerous books written on the subject. Suffice it here to say that the theory of macroevolution violates almost a dozen known laws of science including the second law of thermodynamics, the fact that inorganic material cannot produce organic material, and the law of probability. In addition, scientist have finally recognized the fact that mutations never result in the creation of new DNA information. The addition of new DNA is essential to the theory of macroevolution. Not even a single-celled organism can move up the evolutionary chain without new and different DNA being added. But the mutation process *never* results in a mutation having any additional DNA information. In fact, just the opposite takes place – mutations *always* end up with equal or less genetic material. The results of mutation are defects, deformity, disease, and death but *never* new genetic material.

This is confirmed by the biophysicist Dr Lee Spetner, who taught at Johns Hopkins University:

> "In all the reading I've done in the life-sciences literature, I've never found a mutation that added information .... The NDT [neoDarwinian theory] is supposed to explain how the information of life has been built up by evolution. The essential biological difference between a human and a bacterium is in the information they contain. All other biological differences follow from that. The human genome has much more information than does the bacterial genome. Information

cannot be built up by mutations that lose it. A business can't make money by losing it a little at a time."[4]

Ernst Mayr, a famous evolutionist, thought mutations would explain how evolution took place but his own experiments with fruit flies proved just the opposite! Despite years of experimenting with genetic changes, the only changes that took place were in the structure of the flies. He was able to create fruit flies with more legs or wings or with parts protruding from places they aren't normally attached to. But none of the changes resulted in the formation of any new DNA information which would be required to form a new species. Nothing evolved from his experiments other than fruit flies and even they were left without any improvements to their survival.

Pierre Grasse, known as the greatest scientist in France, wrote, "No matter how numerous they may be, mutations do not produce any kind of evolution."[5] Professor Nils Heribert-Nilsson of Lund University has said, "There is no single instance where it can be maintained that any of the mutants studied has a higher vitality than the mother species." Nilsson added, "It is therefore, absolutely impossible to build a current evolution on mutations or on recombinations."[6]

Michael Pitman, former chemistry professor at Cambridge, confessed, "Neither observation nor controlled experiment has shown natural selection manipulating mutations so as to produce a new gene, hormone, enzyme system or organ."[7] The co-holder of the 1945 Nobel Prize for developing penicillin, Sir Ernest Chain, called natural selection and chance mutations a "hypothesis based on no evidence and irreconcilable with the facts."[8]

All this to say, the Bible has never been proven to be scientifically inaccurate but some of the *theories* of science have. Despite this fact, those who dare question any of these theories are said to be people who do not believe in science. But, again, it is not scientific facts that are being questioned, but the unsubstantiated *hypotheses* that scientists make. Nevertheless, many people have been convinced that anyone who rejects a *postulate* made by a scientist is an ignorant Bible believing religious fanatic who stands in the way of scientific advancement. But nothing could be further from the truth. Many of the world's greatest scientists were Bible believing Christians including Newton, Pasteur, Kepler, Paschal, Fleming, and Edwards.

It is fashionable for skeptics to consider themselves brilliant simply because they question anything spiritual. Dallas Willard, while a professor of philosophy at the University of Southern California made the following observation: "We live in a culture that has, for centuries now, cultivated the idea that the *skeptical* person is always smarter than one who believes. You can be almost as stupid as a cabbage, as long as you *doubt*."[9]

I have heard very arrogant individuals say, "Christians are so ignorant they still believe in a flat earth." Actually, had people read and believed the Bible they would have discovered the earth was round long before Christopher Columbus sailed the ocean blue. Isaiah 40:22, which was written thousands of years before 1492, informs us that God "sits enthroned above the circle of the earth." It was ignorant scientists, and not the scientifically accurate writers of the Bible, who taught the earth was flat. God informed man the earth was round long before any humans figured it out. This is true of many scientific facts found in the Bible. There was a time when medical scientists believed that the best way to cure a diseased patient was through blood-letting (draining blood out of the person's body). Had these "physicians" read and trusted the Bible they would have known better. Written thousands of years earlier, the Bible told us that "the life of every creature is its blood" (Leviticus 17:14). It is the scientists who are found to be wrong over and over again as new and more revealing discoveries are made that disprove their older theories and, at the same time, prove the Bible was accurate all along.

When the beautiful black sand beach on the Big Island of Hawaii was overrun by lava from the volcano, scientists said it would be a long time before anyone would ever see another black sand beach. They estimated it took years to produce such a beach. A few months later, however, a new black sand beach had been created by the very volcano that had wiped out the previous one.

Apparently, when the hot lava flows into the cold ocean water it can quickly break up into tiny particles as it cools, thus creating black sand. This sand can then wash up on shore and in very little time create a new black beach. Imagine the chagrin of the scientists who emphatically stated it would take several years.

Likewise, the faces of scientists today who teach the theory of macroevolution as fact should be red with embarrassment. The massive amount of recent and not-so-recent evidence that the theory is totally fraudulent should leave them nonplussed. Unfortunately, most scientists are not deterred and continue to shamelessly extol the theory as fact. This theory is now so engrained into the fabric of our society, anyone who questions it is labeled unscientific. The truth is that while the Bible is 100% accurate, scientists are not.

The Koran

Let us now consider the Koran with as much sensitivity to its adherents as possible. I will not make any attacks on Islam's holy book, but I will point out facts that are true and should not be denied even if these facts do not reflect positively on the Koran.

At the outset, it must be stated that there are a number of major differences between the Koran and the Bible. For instance, the Koran does not contain fulfilled prophecies from ancient times. The Koran was not written over thousands of years, so there were no earlier predictions of the prophet Mohammad's birth, his teachings, or his manner of death. No manuscripts exist that prophesied events that would take place hundreds of years later with perfect accuracy.

Additionally, the Koran records historical events that contradict what the authors of the Bible record as having happened. This means, of course, if one is true then the other cannot be. The Bible, for example, tells us Christ was crucified. The Koran, on the other hand, says Christ was not crucified. The historical records support the Bible.

Furthermore, the Koran contains some scientific inconsistencies. One example is the Koran's statements about how man came into existence. In Qur'an 6:2 and 7:12 it says man was made from clay. Qur'an 25:54, however, says man was made from water. Then in Qur'an 96:1 it says man was made from a clot of blood. One cannot be sure from reading the Koran what man was originally made from.

Unlike the Koran, the Bible is consistent in describing how man came into being. Genesis 2:7 tells us, "the Lord God formed a man from the dust of the ground and breathed into his nostrils the breath of life, and the man became a living being." This account of how man was created remains the same from the first book of the Bible (Genesis) to the last book of the Bible (Revelation). Not once in either the Old or New Testaments does the Bible claim man was created from something other than the dust of the ground. In the New Testament, for example, we find Paul declaring, "The first man was of the dust of the earth" (1 Corinthians 15:47).

Biblical contradictions

Despite the consistencies, there are Muslims who claim there are contradictions in the Bible. One Muslim writer, Shabbir Ally, wrote a pamphlet entitled *101 Clear Contradictions in the Bible*.[10] When examined closely, however, the contradictions cited were not real but were based on improper interpretations, inaccurate exegesis, and the removal of passages from their context. Knowledgeable scholars have written refutations to all of these supposed Biblical contradictions. Jay Smith, Alex Chowdhry, Toby Jepson, and James Schaeffer wrote a book about them entitled *101 Cleared-Up Contradictions in the Bible* in response to Mr. Ally.[11] Among other things, they explained that:

-he misunderstood the historical context
  25 times
-he misread the text 15 times
-he misunderstood the Hebrew usage 13
  times
-he failed to see that the texts are
actually
  compatible when understood correctly
  13 times
-he misunderstood the author's intent
  12 times
-he did not identify accurately copyist
  error 9 times
-he misunderstood how God works in
  history 6 times
-he misunderstood the Greek usage
  4 times
-he didn't read the entire text 4 times
-he misquoted the text 4 times
-he misunderstood the wording 3 times
-he had too literalistic an interpretation
  3 times
-he imposed his own agenda 3 times
-he confused an incident with another
  1 time
-we now have discovered an earlier
    manuscript 1 time

(You will note that when you add up the totals there are more than 101. That's because Shabbir many times made more than one error in a given question.)

There are many other differences between the Koran and the Bible, but I do not wish to add any more lest I appear to only be interested in discrediting the Koran or maligning Mohammad. That is not my intention. My sincere desire it to present facts, especially to my Muslim friends, in the hope that they will be able to see the truth and reject the lies they have been taught.

CHAPTER 3: MOHAMMAD AND JESUS

One of the most surprising things I discovered about Islam is that it teaches something about Jesus that cannot possibly be true. According to Islam, Jesus was a great prophet. But that is impossible because he claimed to be God Himself. Either Jesus was telling the truth or he was lying. If he *was* telling the truth, then he was far more than just a great prophet. If he *was not* telling the truth, then he was a pathetic liar and certainly not a great prophet. Either way, because of whom he claimed to be, he cannot be viewed as merely a great prophet.

Like every other religious leader, Mohammad was born a mere mortal. He himself never claimed to be a god or to have come directly from God. He never brought anyone back from the dead to show he was divine. By his own admission, he was not sinless from the day he was born until the day he died. He never rose from the dead nor had followers who believed they saw him alive again after he had died. Like all religious leaders who came before him and all those who have come after him, Mohammad claimed to have found the way to God (Allah) and then died and was buried.

By extreme contrast, Jesus actually claimed to be God. In front of his disciples, he told Thomas, "If you really know me, you will know my Father as well. From now on, you do know him and have seen him" (John 14:7). Philip then asked Jesus to show him the Father (vs. 8). Jesus responded, "Don't you know me, Philip, even after I have been among you such a long time? Anyone who has seen me has seen the Father" (vs. 9).

People then, as now, refused to believe Jesus was God in the flesh. John 5:18 tells us people sought to kill him because he was "making himself equal with God." John 8:58 records that the Jews took up stones to kill Jesus because he said, "before Abraham was born, I am!" Notice he did not say before Abraham was born, I *was*. He used the words "I am" to make it clear to the Jews that he was saying he was the God who told Moses "I am who I am" (Exodus 3:14). Again, in the tenth chapter of John, we find the Jews picking up stones to stone Jesus because they said, "you, a mere man, claim to be God" (vs. 33). They did this after he said, "I and the Father are one" (vs. 30).

Unlike any other religious leader, Jesus did not say he found the way to God. Instead, he said he *was* God. This claim is not only unique but astounding! Imagine if someone today announced to the world that he was God in the flesh. He would be considered insane and quickly placed in an asylum. Yet, this is exactly what Jesus claimed.

Jesus

C. S. Lewis, an atheist who became a Christian, said this claim by Jesus leaves us with some inescapable conclusions.[12] Either Jesus is or isn't God. If Jesus isn't really God, he either knew it or he didn't. Thus, he was either a liar (if he knew he wasn't God but pretended to be) or he was a lunatic (if he didn't know he wasn't God but thought he was).

If he knew he was not God, then we are forced to conclude that Jesus was the greatest con artist who ever lived, an evil man and a deliberate deceiver of his followers. He continued to scam people right up until he died, which also makes him a fool. He let people kill him for his false claims, knowing full well they weren't true. It's hard to believe he would allow himself to be crucified for claiming to be God when he knew all along it was a lie. But the way Jesus lived his life and the way he cared for people make it almost impossible to conclude he was evil and knowingly lied about being God.

A second option, and perhaps a more believable possibility, is that he was not God but only thought he was. In this case, Jesus must be viewed as someone who should have been locked up in a padded cell like people who believe they are Napoleon Bonaparte or Jesus Christ. But again, if you look at the rest of the way Jesus conducted himself, you can't conclude Jesus was crazy. He always seemed to have it together and be in complete control, even more so than those around him.

If Jesus was neither a liar nor a lunatic, then we are left with only one other option – He is everything he said he was. He is Lord. Looking at what he did, how he lived his life, and all the circumstantial evidence, this is the only one of the three options that makes sense. There are only three possible reasons why anyone would claim to be God. Jesus was a liar, a lunatic, or Lord. If Jesus is, indeed, God then *we* have two choices: 1. We can accept him as Lord and follow him or 2. We can reject him and consequently become fools ourselves. The following diagram shows the reasoning C. S. Lewis used in determining whether or not Jesus was telling the truth.

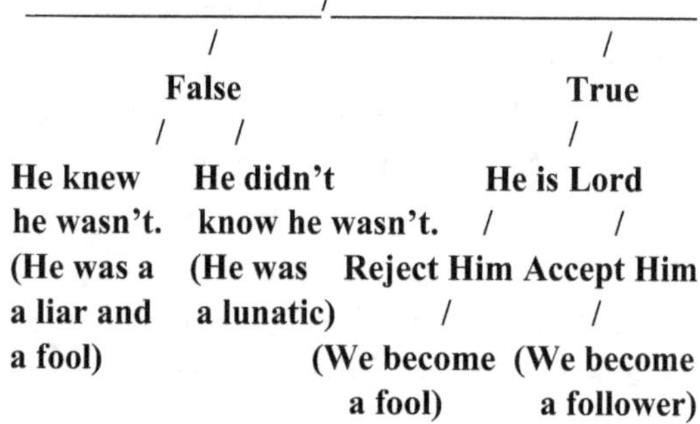

If Jesus is not God Himself, as he claimed, then he had to be either a liar or a lunatic, but he never could have been what Muslims say he was – a great prophet.

Unlike other prophets such as Mohammad, Christ did not say "Here is the way to God." He said *He* was the way. We must decide if we should believe him when he said, "I am the way and the truth and the life. No one comes to the Father except through me" (John 14:6). Acts 4:12 states, "Salvation is found in no one else, for there is no other name under heaven given to mankind by which we must be saved."

If this is true, then no other religious leader (not Mohammad, Buddha, Gandhi, or anyone else) can offer us another way to heaven. If Christ is the only way, then every other way is excluded. We have but two choices – either Christ alone is the way or he must be viewed as a deceiver unfit to be followed.

How does one decide if Jesus was telling the truth, especially about being

God and the only way to heaven? One way to determine his truthfulness is to examine his life. Did he live up to the perfect standard that God would live up to? According to eye witnesses he did. The Apostle Paul said Jesus "had no sin" (2 Corinthians 5:21). The Apostle Peter, who spent years with Jesus, also said, "He committed no sin, and no deceit was found in his mouth" (I Peter 2:22).

Hebrews 7:26 tells us that Jesus was "holy, blameless, pure, set apart from sinners, exalted above the heavens." Those who knew Jesus testified that he never sinned. We know it is impossible for any human being to be sinless their entire life, so anyone who is perfect their whole life must be more than a mere human. They must be God. And that is who Jesus said he was.

If that is true, then Jesus supersedes Mohammad. As a result, we should follow Jesus instead of a mere mortal. It is always better to follow God than any human. We select a doctor on the basis of how good he or she is and their knowledge of medicine. We take our automobile to the automotive repairmen we believe knows best how to take care of our vehicle. The same should be true when it comes to our souls. We should follow the advice of the one we believe knows best how to take care of our souls. Even more, we should trust the one who created our souls. If Jesus was correct when he said he was God, then there is no question as to whose advice we should follow. In examining all the various religious leaders who said they knew the way to God, Jesus stands alone. No one else ever did the things he did or make the claims he did. Consider the many differences between Jesus and Mohammad or any other religious leader.

Jesus Christ	Mohammad (Buddha, Gandhi, or anyone not Christ)
His arrival was prophesied by many writers many years before he came.	No prophecies were written foretelling his coming.
He fulfilled every prophecy written about him.	He didn't fulfill any prophecies as there were none.

He claimed to be God.	He never claimed to be God.
He performed miracles including raising the dead.	He did not raise anyone from the dead.
He was perfect (sinless) throughout his life.	He was not perfect throughout his life and admitted it.
He claimed he came to earth to die for man's sins.	He never claimed he would die for human sin.
He rose from the dead and ascended into heaven alive.	He died and is still dead.
He has entered and continues to enter the hearts of multitudes of people.	He is dead.
He communicates with his followers.	He is dead.
He performs miracles even today.	He is dead.
He has a personal relationship with	He is dead.

each of his followers
on an ongoing basis.

He promised to   He is dead.
return to earth
to raise all men
from the grave.

CHAPTER 4: PARADISE AND HEAVEN

According to the Koran, paradise is a place where men will enjoy being sexually serviced for all eternity by numerous virgins. Will that be paradise for the virgins or the men's wives? It has been suggested that Mohammad taught this in order to recruit young men to serve in his army. I will not assume to know what Mohammad's motives were, but it certainly would make sense. Adolescents whose testosterone levels are so high it affects their thinking would be extremely susceptible to such teaching. It is interesting to note that the Koran says little about what paradise will be like for women. Could that be because women did not serve in Mohammad's army, so there was no need to incentivize them to become followers? Mohammad believed the primary function of women is to provide for the personal pleasure of men, both in this life and the next. Whether it is raising the man's children, taking care of his house, or satisfying him sexually, a woman's happiness is to be found in what can only be described as *servitude*. Thus, it is only reasonable that the Koran would be silent on what women would enjoy in paradise. Are women going to enjoy watching their husbands, sons, and fathers pacifying their unbridled lusts with multiple other women?

It is not with malicious intent that I make what appears to me to be an obvious observation. I think any unbiased person would make the same assessment. It appears to me that the theology Mohammad espoused had a very shallow view of paradise. How does the idea that men will have nothing more important to do forever than satisfying their sexual appetites indicate a faith with much spiritual depth? Such behavior consists of pure selfishness. It is narcissism in its rawest form. Why would a deeply religious person think that physical intercourse is the highest level of spiritual attainment? Rather than leading to increased righteousness, such behavior should lead to increased shame.

And where is Allah all this time? Does he spend eternity just watching all the copulation taking place as an uninvolved voyeur with little else to do? The God of Mohammad appears to be a god whose primary interest is in satisfying the physical needs of men rather than their spiritual needs. Allah is nothing like the God of the Bible who desires for men and women to have meaningful relationships both with Him and with each other. He offers men far more than the simple satisfaction of their sex glands. He also has far more to offer women than servitude to men.

Islam may be unique in its teaching on heaven, but it is not unique in its teaching on how one gets there. Every religion in the world offers some form of eternal bliss for its followers. And in every case, except for Christianity, eternity is obtained by earning it. Whether it is following the eightfold path to Nirvana as taught by Buddhism, gaining enough good karma to be reincarnated upward into the World Soul taught by Hinduism, or keeping all the commandments to gain heaven as taught by Judaism, man must strive to accomplish enough while on earth to warrant a positive afterlife. Eternal bliss is obtained only after one has proven himself or herself worthy enough.

Acceptable to God

By contrast, Christianity teaches that no one can ever be righteous enough to gain heaven. We are all sinful, separated from God, and unable to do anything about it. Romans 3:10 tells us "There is no one righteous, not even one." Isaiah 64:6 also explains that "all our righteous acts are like filthy rags." No matter how much we try to be good enough to gain a spot in heaven, we fall short. Romans 3:23 informs us that "all have sinned and fall short of the glory of God." As a result, unlike every other religion, God does for us what we cannot do for ourselves. He creates a way for us to gain eternal life without us having to earn it.

We do not become acceptable to God by anything we do (religious or otherwise). According to Paul even sacrificing our life for God will not make us more righteous. In fact, by itself, it will do us absolutely no good whatsoever. He writes in I Corinthians 13:3, "Though I give my body to be burned, and have not love, it profiteth me nothing" (KJV). No matter how many good deeds we do, how faithful we are to follow a holy book, or how religious we are, it will not make us right with God.

Only the Christian God loves us so much, He saves us even though we do not deserve to be saved. Christianity alone offers paradise to the totally unrighteous. The Bible says it is not up to us to earn heaven because Jesus earned it for us. Titus 3:5 declares, "He saved us, not because of righteous things we had done, but because of his mercy." Rather than requiring us to be righteous enough for God to accept us, God makes us righteous through his grace and mercy alone. No other religion offers such good news. Because we cannot get to God, God came to us in the form of Jesus Christ.

Muslims have a high and exalted view of Allah, which is good. But such a view also includes a huge separation between Allah and his followers. My

Muslim friends cannot fathom anyone having a personal and intimate relationship with Allah. And because Allah is so great, he certainly would never lower himself to become a man.

This is one of the reasons my Muslim friends cannot accept the idea that Jesus was both God and man. But that is who the Bible tells us Jesus was. For example, in Philippians 2:6-8 we read this about Jesus: "Who, being in very nature God, did not consider equality with God something to be used to his own advantage; rather, he made himself nothing by taking the very nature of a servant, being made in human likeness. And being found in appearance as a man, he humbled himself by becoming obedient to death—even death on a cross!"

The Christian God is more interested in showing how much he loves us than he is in showing us how awesome he is. He was even willing to humble himself and become a man in order to demonstrate how much he loves us. The Bible tells us that he loved us so much that he gave his only begotten son [Jesus] so that those who believe in him would not perish but have everlasting life (John 3:16).

Everyone needs love. Everyone searches for love. Unfortunately, we never have that need met completely by other people because they too are in need of love as much as we are. They too are hoping to find perfect unconditional love from us, but we are incapable of providing it. No one ever receives the love they need from other people because no one is able to give it. If we cannot give it then we can't expect to ever receive it. Man is simply too selfish to give to others what he himself desperately seeks.

So where does one turn to have this great need met? The need is met only by the one who created the need within us in the first place. He is the only one capable of giving us the perfect love we long for. He doesn't just show love. He *is* love. The Bible confirms to us that God is more than just a loving God. He *is* love (1 John 4:16). If we compare Jesus with everyone else who has claimed to have spiritual knowledge of God, we find Jesus was far more loving than any of them. More than just loving others and telling people to love one another, He is love itself. Only He exemplified perfect love throughout His entire life. He alone claimed He could satisfy our need for love.

Furthermore, He demonstrated love in ways no one ever has. He died for mankind so mankind would not have to die. In the Bible we find these words of Jesus, "Greater love has no one than this: to lay down one's life for one's friends" (John 15:13). But Jesus *was* able to demonstrate greater love than man because he laid down his life for more than just his friends. He died for everyone including his *enemies*. The Bible says, "Very rarely will anyone die for a righteous person, though for a good person someone might possibly dare to die. But God demonstrates his own love for us in this: While we were still sinners, Christ died for us." (Romans 5:7-8). Even after being spat upon, beaten, crowned with thorns, and nailed to a cross, He said, "Father, forgive them; for they know not what they do" (Luke 23:34). Never has such amazing love been demonstrated. That

kind of love is found only in God
Himself.

You don't know me.

The majority of those who read this
book will not know me and most will
probably not be interested in knowing
me. But suppose you were walking
across a busy street one day and I
suddenly came running from the curb to
push you out of the way of an
oncoming truck. Suppose that while in
the act of saving your life, I was unable
to save mine. While enabling you to
narrowly escape, I was hit and killed.
You lived because I died for you. How
would you feel toward me then? What
would your attitude be about knowing
who I was after realizing what I had
done? You would have to be an
especially coldhearted person to just
ignore such a compassionate deed.

But this is exactly what Jesus has
done for us. He died that we might live.
Some are unaware of the great sacrifice
Jesus made by dying on the cross on
our behalf. But many others have
simply chosen not to believe what he

did ever happened. Are such people not cold-hearted if they do not, at the very least, check the evidence to see if that is, indeed, what Jesus did? If we discover that the evidence shows that he did take the punishment that we deserve on himself, then we cannot simply ignore it. If we do, then we cannot blame God if he does not forgive us for our sins.

Heaven

So, how does Islam's concept of paradise compare with Christianity's concept of heaven. The biggest difference is found in how we enjoy relationships with God and others. Unlike, Islam's paradise where God is too austere to have a personal relationship with, heaven for Christians will be a place where they love and are loved by their creator. God will commune with his people in the way he did with Adam and Eve in the Garden of Eden before the Fall. He will show us things we have never seen before. He will teach us things we never knew before. But most importantly, he will love us in ways we have never experienced before.

In return, we will keep the two greatest commandments Jesus ever gave us. One is to "'Love the Lord your God with all your heart and with all your soul and with all your mind.' And the second is like it: 'Love your neighbor as yourself'" (Matthew 22:37-39). In other words, we will enjoy being loved by God and friends as well as finding joy in loving God and others. Our love relationships will not be merely physical in nature but supernatural. Just being in fellowship with God and everyone around us will be joy unspeakable and full of glory. We will not be in need of constant sexual arousals to find happiness. Being with Jesus will be more than enough.

CHAPTER 5: LAW AND LOVE

To be a Muslim, one must obey Sharia Law. Sharia law divides offences into two general categories: "hadd" offences, which are serious crimes with set penalties, and "tazir" crimes, where the punishment is left to the discretion of the judge. Hadd offences include theft, which can be punishable by amputating the offender's hand, and adultery, which can carry the penalty of death by stoning.

Muslims believe that following Sharia Law is more important than almost anything else they do. This is evidenced by the fact that Muslim fathers have been known to kill a son or daughter who converts to Christianity. If a daughter becomes pregnant out of wedlock, she may be killed. If a son is discovered to be living a homosexual lifestyle, he too may be killed. Even for minor offenses, Muslim fathers will disown their own flesh and blood regardless of the amount of pleading for forgiveness that may be offered by his son or daughter. Even if the child admits to making a mistake, there is no forgiveness offered. Instead, the laws of Islam demand that the father never again even acknowledges the child's existence. As a result, Muslim sons and daughters obey their parents primarily out of fear.

By contrast, Christian fathers want nothing more than to restore every broken relationship which might occur with his children no matter how grievous their acts may have been. This is also what the God of Christianity wants. This is the kind of love God has for us and wants us to have as well. Even though we have sinned against him, he is willing to forgive. All we have to do is ask for his forgiveness.

Jesus demonstrated this while he was still walking the earth by telling the following parable recorded in Luke 15:11-24:

> "There was a man who had two sons. The younger one said to his father, 'Father, give me my share of the estate.' So, he divided his property between them.

Not long after that, the younger son got together all he had, set off for a distant country and there squandered his wealth in wild living. After he had spent everything, there was a severe famine in that whole country, and he began to be in need. So, he went and hired himself out to a citizen of that country, who sent him to his fields to feed pigs. He longed to fill his stomach with the pods that the pigs were eating, but no one gave him anything.

When he came to his senses, he said, 'How many of my father's hired servants have food to spare, and here I am starving to death! I will set out and go back to my father and say to him: Father, I have sinned against heaven and against you. I am no longer worthy to be called your son; make me like one of your hired servants.' So, he got up and went to his father.

But while he was still a long way off, his father saw him and was filled with compassion for him; he ran to his son, threw his arms around him and kissed him. The son said to him, 'Father, I have sinned against heaven and against you. I am no longer worthy to be called your son.'

But the father said to his servants, 'Quick! Bring the best robe and put it on him. Put a ring on his finger and sandals on his feet. Bring the fattened calf and kill it. Let's have a feast and celebrate. For this son of mine was dead and is alive again; he was lost and is found.' So, they began to celebrate."

What Jesus was illustrating was the way God, the Heavenly Father, loves and forgives. Even though we turn our backs on God and have nothing to do with him, he longs for our return to him. If we "come to our senses" like the prodigal son, the Heavenly Father welcomes us back with open arms.

It would appear that there are three kinds of love. One might be called "if" love. It says, "*If* you love me, then I will love you." You must go first. Then there is what might be called "but" love. It says, "I will love you, *but* you better prove yourself worthy of my love." You must do certain things to keep being loved.

Finally, there is "anyway" love. It says, "No matter what I will love you *anyway*." There is nothing you can do or not do to cause this love to be lost. This is the kind of love that Jesus is. Jesus says, "Disobey me, curse me, spit on me, nail me to a cross, crucify me – I will love you anyway." This cannot be said of Mohammad because Sharia Law demands punishment for sin. Keeping the law is more important than loving others.

Whether you are a Muslim, a Christian, or an atheist there are basically three things that motivate people to action.

Fear

The first is *Fear*, the worst of the three motivators. Whether it is fear of failure, fear of punishment, fear of looking bad, fear of losing something or someone, many people live their entire lives out of fear. They get up every morning and go to work for fear of being fired if they don't. They don't rob a bank for fear of being caught and sent to jail if they do. They take care of their children for fear of being considered a bad parent or out of fear of losing the children's love or even of losing the children themselves. Whatever they do, they do primarily out of fear.

Likewise, whatever they don't do, they don't do out of fear: fear of God, fear of what people might do or say about them, fear of being hurt, fear of not succeeding, or any number of other fears that keep them from even trying, especially something new. Living in fear is a very unhappy way to live; yet, there are many sad people who go through life motivated by fear. The question they ask themselves when making a decision about what they should do is "what can I *lose*?"

Hope

The second motivator for people, the next level up if you will, is *hope*. Social workers spend a great deal of time trying to instill hope in the hopeless. Hope is certainly better than fear, but hope as a sole motivator for living does not result in happiness either.

These people get up in the morning (or perhaps evening) and go to work in the hope of earning enough money to pay their bills, getting a promotion and/or raise (climbing the corporate ladder), providing their family with a sense of financial security, or perhaps in the hope of purchasing a particular desired object such as a house, car, or dream vacation trip. These people do what they do in the hope of getting ahead, taking advantage of every opportunity, or perhaps seeing what they can accumulate by way of wealth and what it can buy. The question for people motivated by hope is "what can I *gain*?"

Muslim extremists, like *The Five Percenters,* appear to be motivated by anger and hate. But these attitudes result in behavior that is also motivated by hope. Whether it is the hope of getting revenge for wrongs done to them, the joy of killing infidels, or the knowledge they are pleasing Allah by destroying Christians and Jews, the ultimate reason for their actions is hope of reward. Being driven by anger and hate causes one to do things one hopes will result in some kind of personal satisfaction or gain either in this life or the next.

All religions offer some form of hope. But what separates Christianity from all others is that hope for eternal life is not based on anything man does. Christians realize their hope is based solely on what Jesus did for them on the cross.

Love

The final motivator, the highest level, is *love*. The question asked by people motivated by love is "what can I *give*?" People motivated by love live their lives meeting the needs of others rather than being concerned about making sure their own needs are met. They look for opportunities to serve rather than worrying about whether they are getting their fair share. They even love their enemies.

In summary, everyone is motivated by one of these three motivators:

Fear – What can I lose?
Hope – What can I gain?
Love – What can I give?

It appears to me that Muslims are motivated by the belief that Islam is the only true religion and they will be eternally rewarded if they follow the teachings of Mohammad. Thus, they are primarily motivated by hope. They may also be motivated by fear if they think Allah will punish them if they do not do what he requires.

True Christians, on the other hand, have no need to be afraid of their God because they know he loves them. John 3:17 tells us that "God did not send his Son into the world to condemn the world, but to save the world through him." Knowing they are loved and accepted by God, Christians are not motivated by fear but by love. They know that of all the things that will last forever, love is the greatest (I Corinthians 13:13). Christianity teaches that the most important thing in life is to love God and others.

The Bible says, "If I have the gift of prophecy [or even if I am a prophet] and can fathom all mysteries and all knowledge, and if I have a faith that can move mountains, but have not love, I am nothing" (1 Corinthians 13:2).

Jesus instructed His followers to "Love your enemies, bless them that curse you, do good to them that hate you, and pray for them which despitefully use you, and persecute you" (Matthew 5:44 KJV).

This instruction by Jesus explains why Christian doctors go to Muslim countries to meet the needs of the poor who are sick and injured. They volunteer and charge the poor nothing for their services. Christian hospitals are built in Muslim countries to provide medical treatment for those who would not otherwise receive it. Christian organizations supply food, medicine, and other assistance to those in need regardless of their religious beliefs. The reason for all this compassion from Christians is not to gain eternal rewards but simply to love as they have been loved by their God. They serve Christ out of love and gratitude for what He has done for them.

It is not unlike the way children respond in love for parents who love them. For example, suppose an earthly father goes out for an evening, leaving his teenage son home alone. If the father and son love each other, the father doesn't need to tell his son not to trash the house while he is gone. He knows his son would not be so disobedient. The son would not even consider trashing his father's house. His actions (or nonactions) are not based on the fear of receiving a beating when his father returns or of getting paid for his good behavior. No, it is because he has no desire to disrespect his father whom he loves. Of course, a good father does not beat his son, so there is no fear of that happening in the son's mind anyway. Love, not fear or desire for reward, determines the son's behavior.

Stone throwing

Let me share another illustration that will help explain this concept. Imagine there are two glass houses built on the same street, but one had a sign in the yard that read: "DO NOT THROW STONES!" Which house do you think would have a stone thrown at it first? The one with the sign saying "DO NOT" of course.

Something inside every one of us tempts us to see if we can get away with throwing a stone. Something in us doesn't want to be told what we can and can't do. Something in us wants to be able to get away with rebelling against the rules. Something in us tells us it would probably be a lot of fun to try. Without the sign we might not even have thought of stone throwing. But the sign created a new attitude toward the house that was not there before. All of a sudden, the sign reminds us of the saying, "Rules (and perhaps glass houses) are made to be broken." We might even believe that whoever would put up such a sign is just asking for trouble. The sign and its orders actually increase the probability of stones being thrown. This is true of all laws.

God knew this principle even when He issued His commandments. Romans

5:20 points out "the law entered that sin might abound." The commandments show us how inept we are in being good in our own efforts. It is our complete inability to keep God's commandments that reveals our imperfection, not our perfection, and causes us to seek God for His forgiveness, His righteousness, and His love.

Now what would be the best way to stop a determined individual from throwing stones at a particular glass house? The owner could set up an elaborate alarm system on the lawn, hire a twenty-four-hour security guard, or go to the extent of getting laws passed that would increase the punishment for stone throwers. And while all these things would no doubt serve as deterrents to even the most determined stone throwers, they would not change the desire of the stone thrower to hurl stones at the house. Even though they might be good ideas and good laws, the potential stone thrower's heart and mind remain unchanged.

What would actually change the stone thrower's desire to throw stones at the house? What if you moved that person's family or a friend he loved very much into the house? Because of the stone thrower's love for the people living in the house, he would no longer have the desire to throw stones. He would not want to hurt the ones he loves. Thus, what more laws and regulations could not do, love would accomplish.

Now the stone thrower refrains from throwing stones, not because the law commands it, but because his heart is changed. The law is no longer needed because love would not even think of destroying a loved one's home. Nor are security guards and alarm systems necessary. The old way of dealing with the criminal and his crime is replaced with a new and better way. This is the way it is with God's commandments. A desire to keep from breaking commandments is not created through fear of punishment or hope of reward. The desire comes from a love for and trust in the giver of the commandments. Thus, obedience is not based on a sense of *duty* but on a *desire* created from our love for and trust in God. The Bible says "we love him because he first loved us" (1 John 4:19).

If you obey God out of fear, you do not have the right relationship with him for there is no fear in love. 1 John 4:18 tells us, "There is no fear in love. But perfect love drives out fear, because fear has to do with punishment. The one who fears is not made perfect in love."

CHAPTER 6: ABSOLUTES AND TOLERANCE

Our postmodern society has decided nothing is absolutely true. Today, the phrase often heard is, "there are no absolutes." This is ironic, if not comical, because the very statement "there are no absolutes" is stating an absolute. Anytime someone asserts an idea to be categorically true, he is claiming an absolute. Therefore, the statement "there are no absolutes" is by definition false because in order to be true the statement itself would have to be an absolute. In other words, you cannot be *absolutely* sure there are no absolutes.

This belief in relativism, however, does not work in the real world. For example, you may choose to believe you can stand on a railroad track and the oncoming train will not hit you. Just because you believe that to be true does not mean it is. The train will, indeed, hit you regardless of what particular belief system you may hold. To ignore the fact there is truth (speeding trains kill) and there is falsehood (I can survive even if hit by a speeding train) is to live in unreality and it is dangerous. In order to make sound judgments (e.g., deciding to avoid speeding trains) it is imperative then one knows the difference between what is true and what is false. To say there is no difference is both dishonest and foolish. Thus, in reality, we all accept the existence of absolute truths.

No one questions, for example, the absolute truth that the shortest distance between two points is a straight line. If you don't think this is an absolute, then I will race you from Atlanta, Georgia, to Macon, Georgia, by going south while you go any other way you choose. If you try to get there by going north, east or west, I guarantee you I will be there before you. This will be absolutely true every time. In fact, you probably will never end up in Macon, Georgia, because you will either get lost somewhere before the North Pole or be continually going around the earth in circles. There are absolute truths.

It is also important to realize we accept things to be true even if we do not fully understand them. Those of us living in the real world believe electricity exists even if we can't fully explain it. It is because we believe in electricity that we avoid sticking our fingers into wall sockets. Likewise, we believe things exist even if we have never personally seen them. Few people have ever seen a virus, yet we still believe they exist and take precautions to avoid them. If I choose to believe that viruses do not exist because I have never seen one, it does not change the reality of their existence. I can deny reality all I want, but it will not change reality. If I do not believe in the existence of viruses and so take no precautions to avoid them, I not only show my ignorance, but I may ultimately pay the price for my foolishness by becoming sick. Such ignorance may even lead to my death. It is imperative, therefore, that we know about and believe in things we cannot see.

The information age

Obviously, we cannot know everything about everything. In the early 1980's, I was taking classes from a well- respected school in an attempt to obtain a master's degree. One course dealt with the information explosion taking place.

In order to convey just how rapidly knowledge was increasing, the professor stated that in the medical field alone there are 40,000 pages of new material published every day. Then he asked, "How many have read today's publications?" One smart aleck in the back of the room yelled out, "I have one more page to go."

The professor's point was very clear. It was impossible to keep up with the increase in knowledge in one area of study (the medical field) to say nothing of the innumerable other areas of information. The reality is we have an extremely limited amount of knowledge compared to the vast amount that exists and the gap continues to grow exponentially.

If we were to take all of the knowledge contained in the entire universe and represent it by a huge circle, how much space in the circle do you, dear reader, think your amount of knowledge would take up? My knowledge would probably best be represented by just a small dot in the circle. Perhaps your knowledge would be more than mine and would be contained in a small circle. Maybe Einstein's knowledge could be shown as a larger circle, but it would still be relatively small in size compared to the whole circle of universal knowledge.

Knowledge Diagram

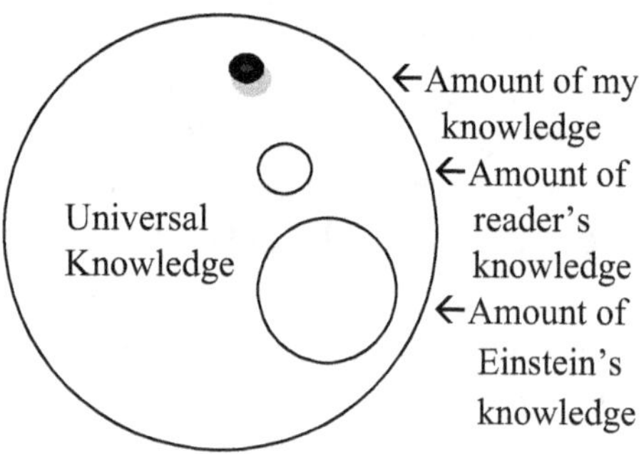

An abundance of ignorance

Because no one knows everything, the honest person is forced to admit there are vast amounts of information, objects, truths, and people totally unknown to him or her. These things are unknown because they exist outside a particular individual's sphere of knowledge.

For example, most readers of this book have no knowledge of my brother, Frank. Not only do you (the reader) know nothing about what he is like, you don't even know if he exists. Because you have never met my brother, you can only trust I am being truthful when I say he exists. I know he does because I have met him personally. I have experienced for myself his big bear hug. Others have the option to accept or not accept the reality of my brother based on my word. If you don't believe I am telling the truth or, perhaps, I am mentally deranged, you will decide he does not exist. If you believe I am credible, you will accept my word for his reality. Either way you decide will have no impact on the absolute truth of his existence. If you ultimately decide he does not exist, then you are basing that belief on total ignorance.

You may, of course, decide you are uncertain of his existence because you have never had any firsthand knowledge of him. What you cannot do, however, is definitively know that he does not exist because he may exist outside your sphere of knowledge. In order to be absolutely certain Frank does not exist, you must believe there is no knowledge beyond what you know. Such a conclusion is the pinnacle of arrogance. You are saying, "I possess ultimate knowledge" and "I know that all those who claim to have met Frank are wrong while I am right." Could there be anything more prideful? Such an absurd position would be like a scientist categorically claiming there are no living organisms anywhere in the universe other than those on the earth. Such a claim would be foolish because the scientist has never visited or examined every planet in every galaxy. Because the scientist knows he lacks universal knowledge, he would never make such a claim.

Suppose the scientist was able to visit other planets and discovered a living organism say on Mars. The organism's existence (like my brother) would be an absolute truth regardless of anyone's thoughts, feelings, or beliefs about it. Truth is not relative simply because I question the veracity of it.

The same is true for the existence of Jesus. If one chooses not to believe me, as well as the millions of people who claim to have had an encounter with Jesus, then one should, at the very least, examine the evidence. Don't be satisfied that he no longer exists simply because you have been told that by others or even that the Koran says so. Search until you find him, because he does exist. I know because I have met him and commune with him daily.

Tolerance

With the postmodernists' rejection of absolute truth came the cry for tolerance. On the surface this seems like the caring thing to do. The problem with this philosophy, however, is that it is not what it appears to be on the surface. Advocating tolerance is a good thing as long as you know what tolerance is.

Tolerance is not the acceptance of everyone's beliefs as equally valid but the acceptance of the right of everyone to believe what they will even though you know they are wrong. In fact, it is only when one is in disagreement with another's view that tolerance is even required. If both parties totally agree, then intolerance is never an issue. But today's advocates for tolerance are seeking something more. They are asking for everyone to accept whatever philosophy others may have. In addition, they are intolerant of those who do not accept their particular brand of tolerance. They are tolerant of everyone except those who believe in absolute truth because those people are wrong and cannot be tolerated.

If tolerance means the acceptance of everyone's beliefs and behavior, including their choice to be murderous, then society will self-destruct. Tolerance must have limits. Intolerance of evil acts such as slavery or genocide is not narrow-mindedness, but responsible behavior. Tolerance for all of mankind's behavior, including the murder of people of tolerance, leads to the end of tolerance itself. Thus, the unlimited tolerance advocated by postmodernists is self- defeating.

Compassion

Furthermore, telling someone he is wrong is not an act of intolerance. Nor does it demonstrate a lack of compassion. *Not* telling someone he is wrong when to remain silent would result in his harm demonstrates a lack of compassion. Telling someone he is wrong to stand in front of an oncoming train is not an act of intolerance. Only when another person is considered of value does one care enough to point out his or her errors. If the other person is of no consequence, then there is no motivation to correct him.

In math we all accept the absolute truth one plus one equals two. We cannot arbitrarily decide to allow one plus one to also equal three, five, and eight – even in the interest of being tolerant or broadminded – because truth is narrow. Because truth is narrow it is cruel not to give the truth to people who believe falsehood, especially if their erroneous thinking could be hurtful to them. A man would have to be a sadist to not warn thirsty people the water they are about to drink is poisonous if he knows it to be true. In this case, ignorance is not bliss but deadly and informing the thirsty people of their potentially lethal mistake (their ignorance) is not intolerance but an act of compassion. It is incumbent upon those who know the truth to try to educate the ignorant, especially if their ignorance is potentially dangerous.

Christ is alive.

Because I know, without a doubt, that Christ is "the way, the truth, and the life" (John 14:6), I have a moral obligation to tell everyone including (perhaps, especially) my Muslim friends. If I do not, I show a complete lack of compassion for their spiritual well-being and eternal destinies. Rather than being intolerant I show I care for others when I tell them about Jesus because I know the consequences of their lack of knowledge. It is for this reason (my loving concern for my lost Muslim friends) that I wrote this book.

NOTES

1. F. F. Bruce, "Archaeological Confirmation of the New Testament." *Revelation and the Bible*, Edited by Carl Henry. (Grand Rapids: Baker Book House, 1969), p. 331.

2. Dr. Nelson Glueck, *Rivers in the Desert*, (New York: Farrar, Strous and Cudahy, 1959), p.136.

3. Dr. Joseph P. Free, *Archaeology and Bible History*, (Wheaton, IL: Scripture Press, 1969), p.1.

4. Dr Lee Spetner, *Not by Chance*, (Brooklyn, NY: The Judaica Press, Inc.), p. 131–132, 138, 143. See review in Creation 20(1):50–51, December 1997–February 1998.

5. Grasse, Pierre-Paul, *Evolution of Living Organisms*, (New York: Academic Press, 1977), p. 88.

6. Professor Nils Heribert-Nilsson, *Synthetische Artbildung* [Synthetic Speciation] (1953), p. 1157.

7. Michael Pitman, *Adam and Evolution*, (London: Rider & Co; First Edition, 1984) *pp. 67-68.*

8. Sir Ernest E. Chain, "Social

Responsibility and the Scientist in Modern Western Society" (Robert Waley Cohen memorial lecture, 1970).

9. Dallas Willard, *Hearing God: Developing a Conversational Relationship With God*, (Illinois: InterVarsity Press, 1999), p. 218.

10. Shabbir Ally, *101 Contradictions in the Bible*, (Canada: Al Attique Publishers, 2001).

11. Jay Smith, Alex Chowdhry, Toby Jepson, James Schaeffer, *101 Cleared-Up Contradictions in the Bible*.

12. C. S. Lewis, *Mere Christianity*, (London: Macmillan Publishers Ltd., 1952).